MEDIEVAL IRISH LYRICS

medieval IRISh Lyrics

Edited and Translated by
BaRBaRa hughes fowler

University of Notre Dame Press
Notre Dame, Indiana

© 2000 by
University of Notre Dame Press
Notre Dame, Indiana 46556
All Rights Reserved
http://www.undpress.nd.edu

Text Design by Richard Hendel
Set in 11.5/14 Monotype Garamond by Stanton Publication Services, Inc.
Printed in the USA by McNaughton & Gunn, Inc.

Library of Congress Cataloging-in-Publication Data

Medieval Irish lyrics / edited and translated by Barbara Hughes Fowler.
    p.   cm.
    Includes bibliographical references.
    ISBN 0-268-03456-7 (alk. paper) — ISBN 0-268-03457-5 (pbk. : alk. paper)
    1. Irish poetry—To 1100—Translations into English. 2. Irish poetry—
Middle Irish, 1100–1550—Translations into English. 3. Irish poetry—Middle
Irish, 1100–1550. 4. Irish poetry—To 1100. 5. Middle Ages—Poetry.
6. Ireland—Poetry. I. Fowler, Barbara Hughes, 1926–2000
PB1424 .M34 2000
891.6'21040801—dc21

                                      00-055979

∞ *This book is printed on acid-free paper*

Contents

Introduction

Ireland was until about 12,000 B.C. uninhabited.[1] The climate was too arctic to support human life. Between about 12,000 and 10,000 B.C. the ice cap receded and so allowed wild horses and great-horned deer to cross over the land bridge from Scotland to Ireland. At about the same time a mesolithic people came to Ireland, perhaps from Britain and Scandinavia. These first Irishmen were small and dark. They left no monuments behind them. We know of them only through their rubbish dumps and the charcoal traces of their campfires. They did use some flint tools.

Three thousand years later a neolithic people arrived in Ireland. These were agriculturists, originally driven out of the Middle East because of expanding populations and soil depletion. They crossed into Ireland about 3700 B.C., probably from France, Cornwall, and the Low Countries. These people too were small and dark. They used stone tools as well as flint arrows and knives. They cleared forests, planted wheat and barley, and pastured sheep and cattle. In time they began to live in settled communities. They buried their dead and built elaborate stone graves for them, the ruins of which can be seen in Ireland today. The most famous of these is the passage grave at Newgate, county Meath, which was built around 2500 B.C.

At the beginning of the Bronze Age (around 2000 B.C.) voyagers came for trade from Spain and Portugal to Brittany, Cornwall, and Ireland. From there they went on to Great Britain and Scandinavia. Spain had contacts too with North Africa, Greece, and the Near East. Irish ornaments in gold and Irish pottery were to be found in markets throughout Europe. In Ireland could be found amber from the Baltic, bronze daggers and axes from Portugal, and faience beads perhaps from Egypt.

Between 2100 and 1300 B.C. a new, round-headed people, completely different from the neolithic people who had preceded them, arrived in Ireland. They were probably Indo-European and came to be known

---

1. The information in this part of my Introduction is taken from Katharine Scherman's charming book *The Flowering of Ireland: Saints, Scholars, and Kings* (Boston, 1981, reprinted 1996), which I enthusiastically recommend to those interested in this surprising culture.

from the pottery they made as the Beaker Folk. Their arrival in Ireland marks the beginning of the Celtic age, which lasted from about 1300 B.C. to about 600 B.C. They brought with them the culture known as La Tène, from the place in Switzerland where their earliest artifacts were found. Theirs was a hierarchical society. At the top of the social scale were the warriors and the druids. The druids were priests, philosophers, teachers, judges, and poets. Just below them came the artists and artisans. The La Tène artists covered stone and metal objects with "intricate designs of arabesques and tendrils entwining fantastical plants, animal faces and figures."[2] They also learned the arts of enameling and of making colored glass, of weaving and dying, and of making weaponry. Druids, who trained for as long as twenty years, taught astronomy, geography, philosophy, law, and religion. Aristocratic children were taught the art of warfare. The La Tène people operated in small groups such as the family *(fine),* which included all male relations in the line of descent for five generations, and the *tuath,* which was a cluster of families ruled by a king elected by the freemen. There were more than one hundred of these petty kingdoms, grouped into five overkingdoms ruled by a high king *(ard-ri)*. The warfare the *tuaths* practiced consisted chiefly of cattle raids against one another. Such was the legendary contest between the provinces of Ulster and Connacht, the story preserved orally until it was written down by monks in the Christian era. This was the *Tain Bo Cuailnge* (Cattle Raid of Cooley). The superhuman Cú Chulainn was the hero of the epic.

The Celts had a complex body of common law called the Brehon Laws. Homicide and bodily injury were punished by a fine called an *eric.* Kings and nobles owned the land. The cow lord *(bo-aire)* owned property but not land. Both nobles and cow lords were free men. The nonfree were laborers, herdsmen, squatters, and fugitives *(fudir)*. No one below the rank of noble could travel outside the *tuath* without special permission. The only people who were allowed to do so were the *aes dana* (people of poetry). These were poets, historians, jurists, physicians, and skilled craftsmen. The master *(ollam)* of any of these arts was the equal of a king. The Celts also had a system of fosterage. Boys and girls were sent out at an early age to live with foster parents who were responsible for their instruction and care.

2. Ibid., 23.

The religion of the Celts is shadowy, chiefly because there are no written records from that period. What knowledge we have comes from the Christian monks, who made the gods mortal. The *Lebor Gabala* (Book of Invasions) is their attempt to fit Irish history into a world history that began with the Old Testament. It describes five invasions of Ireland, the fourth being that of the *Tuatha de Danann* (People of the Goddess Dana). This *Tuatha* had two chief gods: Lug, who really belongs to an earlier pantheon, and Dagda, whose name means "The Good." Dagda's son Ogma was the god of literature; the highest of the *aes dana* were his devotees, the *filid*. This class claimed to go back to the druid Amergin, son of Nil, who chanted a poetic hymn to all the beings of Earth and Sky as he stepped upon Irish soil in the fifth and totally mythical invasion.

The Celts had an alphabet called ogam after the god of literature who invented it. It consists of horizontal or slanting strokes upon a vertical stem for consonants and of dots for vowels, the letters being distinguished by the number of those strokes and dots. It was extremely clumsy and was used therefore chiefly for inscriptions for the dead carved on wood and stone. The Celts played harps, wind and brass instruments, bagpipes, and horns. The horns were used to summon men to war. Artisans wrought "circles, spirals, zigzags, and trumpet shapes"[3] on bronze, gold, iron, wood, and stone. The most famous example of this La Tène art style is the Turoe Stone in county Galway.

A group of stories later than those of Cú Chulainn in the Ulster Cycle was the *Fíana* (tales of Finn Mac Cumaid and his followers). Finn himself was both a hero and a demigod. He and his men were hunters living off the land. Seminomadic, they were attuned and sympathetic to nature. Members of the bands had to foreswear family and home, and then become poets trained in the twelve traditional forms of poetry. They also had to pass rigorous physical tests. Although they lived by hunting, plundering, and warfare, they were not considered brigands but rather the king's defenders, who kept the coasts and harbors free of foreign invaders; they were also seen as friends of the people (see the note on "Cáel Praises Créide's House"). The tales of these bands were recorded by cloistered monks some centuries later. From them we learn

3. Ibid., 37.

that the Fíana wore fantastically beautiful clothing and were weighed down with jewels and gold.

Although Saint Patrick is generally given credit for bringing Christianity to Ireland and for driving the snakes out of it, he did neither. There were at least four holy men before him, and the snakes had left during the Ice Age. These men were Saint Ciaran of Saighir and Ossory, Saint Ailbe of Emly, Saint Ibar of Beg Erin, and Saint Declan of Ardmore. They worked in the south of Ireland in the fourth and fifth centuries A.D. (Saint Ibar founded a monastery on Beg Erin, at that time an island in Wexford Harbor. Students came there from all over Ireland, as did Christians from the Continent who were fleeing the Hun.) In 431 Pope Celestine sent Palladius to strengthen Christianity in Ireland. As Palladius neither spoke the language nor understood the culture, however, he was not very successful. What Saint Patrick brought to Ireland was the Roman alphabet and the knowledge of Latin, and this was to effect an enormous change in the culture. Monks began to write down the stories of the Celtic Heroic Age, and they delighted too in the Roman poets. They could compose verse in both Latin and the vernacular.

Saint Patrick was the son of a British official of the Roman administration, who may himself have been a Christian. He was born about A.D. 390, possibly in the district of the Severn in western Britain. At sixteen he was taken prisoner by the Irish in a raid and sold to a farmer, Milcho of county Antrim. After six years of slavery he sailed to the Continent. There he learned Latin, perhaps in Auxerre, and was ordained a priest. Later he was appointed bishop of the Irish and was sent back to Ireland to propagate the faith. Saint Patrick worked in the north of Ireland. He found the Celts quite amenable to Christianity, and indeed the bishops' sees often coincided with the *tuaths*—They were a good fit.

In about A.D. 480 Saint Enda built his monasterey on the island of Inishmore, county Galway, and later ten sister monasteries, which attracted scholars and holy men from Europe, who carried back with them their admiration for Irish sanctity and scholarship. In A.D. 515 one of Enda's disciples, Saint Finian, founded a monastery at Clonard on the river Boyne, county Meath. Finian, a good administrator and teacher, was to become the patriarch of Irish monasticism. Saint Brigid, born about A.D. 450, founded monasteries for women, the first being in the

Curragh, county Kildare. Her own monastery was coeducational. The very ascetic Saint Kevin built a monastery at Glendalough, county Wicklow, of which little now remains. One of Finian's apostles, Ciaran, born at about A.D. 516, was directed by Enda to found a monastery at Clonmacnoise. Saint Finian's follower Saint Comgall founded a monastery at Bangor, county Down; his monastic rule became one of the eight chief rules of Ireland.

These monasteries were not at all like modern ones. They were in fact little villages of beehive-shaped huts built around a church. Each monk lived alone in his hut, though some monks preferred to live even more alone as hermits in the wilderness. The remains of these huts and churches can be seen throughout Ireland today.

A number of monks went abroad into self-imposed exiles, to return either in old age or not at all. One of the most famous of these was Saint Brendan. The stories of his fabulous journeys into the North Atlantic and perhaps to Iceland or even North America are told in the tenth-century *Navagatio Sancti Brendani*. After seven years of traveling Brendan returned home and founded monasteries in Connacht and Munster; his rule became another of the eight monastic rules of Ireland. Saint Columba of Iona exiled himself to Scotland where he converted the Highlands to Christianity (see note on "A Blue Eye"). He died there on the island of Iona in A.D. 597. Saint Columbanus of Luxeuil, born in Leinster in A.D. 543, exiled himself to the foothills of the Vosges mountains in France near the Swiss and German borders and founded monasteries at Luxeuil, Annegray, and Fontaines. For more than two hundred years the Irish monasteries at home and abroad functioned in relative peace, although they did sometimes engage in fierce battles with one another.

In A.D. 795 a Viking ship landed on the northeast coast of Ireland. Its men sacked and burned the monastery there, which was said to have been founded by Saint Columba. During the rest of the eighth and throughout the ninth century the Vikings continued to rob and destroy the monasteries, which were strongholds of wealth as well as learning. Eventually the Vikings were absorbed by the Irish culture and contributed much to it: the building of better ships, which stimulated fishing and trade, the introduction of coinage, and the founding of cities, such as Dublin and Limerick. The Viking invasions were followed in the twelfth century by those of the Normans which were even more murderous. It was during this period, however, that the monasteries began their great collections of the Irish sagas of the old Celtic culture.

The poems in this book were composed between around A.D. 800 and 1200. They are all anonymous, although some of them are attributed to legendary or historical figures who had died centuries before. They were composed by monks who wrote them in the margins of the manuscripts they were copying or interpolated poems they had either known or composed in the pagan tales they were recording. In some of the poems monks write about themselves and their ascetic ways. Although most lived in the monasteries, some of the monks preferred to live alone in the wilderness and write of the bounty of nature; "King and Hermit" and "Manchán's Wish" are descriptions of this style of life.

Between A.D. 800 and 1200 Irish monks traveled to the Continent to make converts to Christianity. They took with them their astonishing learning in Greek and Latin as well as their beautifully illustrated manuscripts. Proof of this activity can be found in the ninth-century poem "Pangur Ban," which was discovered in a monastery in southern Austria. Irish poets were writing in the vernacular long before other Europeans dreamed of such a thing.

Many of the poems I've chosen to translate have a slight Christian overlay but are for the most part out of dreamland, or "the other-world,"[4] or what the Irish called *Tír na n'Og* (Land of the Young). This was not a place you went after death if you had behaved yourself in life. It was a paradise of lovely women, bountiful food and drink, and endless treasures of silver, gold, and jewels which lay behind the mist, probably of the Atlantic Ocean. It was where the imaginative Irish longed to go, and where some of them may actually have ventured.

"The Island with a Bridge of Glass" appears in an eighth-century version of an ancient pagan tale. It tells of a voyage made in early Christian times, but it is really out of fairyland. "Fair Lady, Will You Go with Me?" is another description of a dreamland. It was composed in the late ninth century, but the tale it tells comes from pagan times. The monk who composed or recorded this poem did make slight concessions to Christianity. The fifth stanza says that in that paradise men and women conceive with neither guilt nor sin. The sixth stanza refers

4. Gerard Murphy, *Early Irish Lyrics* (Oxford, 1956, reprinted 1962, 1970).

to Adam's sin, which by its darkness hides men of today from those who would count them. Another description of such a fairyland occurs in Lóeg's description to Cú Chulainn of Labraid's home in Mag Mell (Plain of Delights). Cú Chulainn was the greatest of the pagan heroes, so the story the poem tells must date from pre-Christian times even though it was composed, probably by a monk, in the late eleventh century.

"Manannán Describes His Kingdom to Bran" is another tale out of the pagan past. Manannán was the god of the sea who traveled over the ocean in a chariot. Legends on the Isle of Man, supposedly named for him, and in parts of Leinster tell of him rolling on three legs like a wheel through the mist. In *Cormac's Glossary,* a tenth-century work attributed to Bishop Cormac Mac Cuilennain, king of Munster, he becomes an accomplished seaman who could predict the weather. It was from his skill as a mariner that the Irish called him a god of the sea. Here is a cleric trying to preserve his Celtic heritage and at the same time pay his respects to Christianity.[5]

Other poems seem to have a firmer basis in fact. The Líadan of "Líadan Tells of Her Love for Cuirithir" is said to have been a poet of the early seventh century, but the poem was composed in ninth-century Irish and is clearly a story of Christian times, since Líadan becomes a nun and her lover Cuirithir a monk. "Créide's Lament for Dínertach" may have some basis in fact, for the battle in which Dínertach died did occur in A.D. 649.

Of the five poems attributed to Mad Suibne, one dates to the ninth century but the others to the twelfth. Suibne is said to have lost his reason at the battle of Mag Rath in A.D. 639. Historical figures and an actual monastery are mentioned in the poem, so the tale certainly comes from the Christian era, but in their descriptions of nature and the bizarre behavior of their characters the poems are far more pagan than Christian in tone.

Another example of the monks' ability to recreate the past in their imaginations is that of the five poems attributed to Colum Cille (Saint Columba), who died in A.D. 597. The poems themselves date to the eleventh and twelfth centuries. Colum Cille was born an aristocrat. He was often in trouble because of his arrogant ways. He copied a book of

5. Scherman, *The Flowering of Ireland,* 151–52.

psalms that belonged to his teacher and friend Finian in spite of Finian's instruction. Books in Ireland had a certain mystique, and priests were inclined to keep their learning to themselves. When Colum Cille refused to give Finian the copy he had made, the two appealed to King Díarmait, who ruled in Finian's favor. Colum Cille then returned the book and the copy to Finian "with conspicuous ill grace."[6] Not long after this episode a son of the king of Connacht killed one of Díarmait's servants in a game of hurling. The penalty for disturbing the peace of the games was death. Díarmait's son fled to Colum Cille, who was his kinsman, for sanctuary, but Díarmait's officers violated the sanctuary and seized the young man. The result was a war in which Díarmait was defeated. The leaders of Colum Cille's faction suggested that he place himself upon the throne of Northern Ireland, but he refused and in remorse for his action exiled himself to Scotland to convert as many souls as had died on his account.[7] The haunting verses attributed to him reveal a poet who in his imagination relived Colum Cille's homesickness.

THE PRONUNCIATION OF OLD IRISH

Although there is no absolute certainty about the pronunciation of Old Irish, we have from reasonable orthographic conventions, loanword evidence, modern pronunciations, and the usual sort of clues to the phonetics of earlier stages of languages quite a clear idea of the pronunciation of Old Irish. The following rules may be of some help. They are taken from E. G. Quin, *Old Irish Workbook* (Dublin, 1975), 1–10. A fuller explanation is given in R. Thurneysen, *A Grammar of Old Irish* (Dublin, 1946), 27–153.

The accent is generally on the first syllable. Acute accents mark a long vowel, not stress.

The diphthongs *ia, ua, eo,* and *iu* may be pronounced as such.

Ai, oi, ui, ei, ái, ói, úi are not always diphthongs. For instance, *ben* and *bein* are pronounced almost alike. So too for *ór* and *óir* and *gabál* and *gabáil*. The *i* marks palatal quality on the following consonant. It is really a *y*-like off-glide to that consonant.

6. Ibid., 152.
7. Ibid., 153.

C, p, and *t* in initial position are pronounced as in English. Thus
cor is pronounced *kor; poc* is pronounced *pog; tol* is pronounced
tol. (The *t* is, however, dental rather than alveolar as in English.)
Between vowels and when in final position after vowels, they
usually are voiced. Thus *bucae* is pronounced *buge; boc* is pro-
nounced *bog; popul* is pronounced *pobul; fotae* is pronounced *fode.*
Note that *ae* is pronounced like the English short *e.*
Ch is pronounced as in Scottish *loch.*
Ph is pronounced as *f.*
Th is pronounced as some but not all English *th*s; that is, in *bath* but
not *bathe.*

EARLY IRISH METERS

The meters of early Irish poetry were based primarily upon syllable
count, but they also had a complicated system of internal and end
rhymes, alliteration, consonance, and assonance. Consonants could
rhyme by classes, such as the voiceless stops *(p, t, c),* the voiced stops *(b,
d, g),* and the fricatives *(ph, th, ch).* Seven-syllable lines were common,
and end rhymes might be by couplets or by alternating lines. Quatrains
were the usual form. Ruth Lehmann *(Early Irish Verse* [Austin, 1982],
introduction) also gives an excellent description of these techniques,
and her own "imitative" translations do give the English-speaking
reader a good sense of what the Irish verse was like. Here, for instance,
is a poem with a typical seven-syllable line. The alliteration and the
consonance are obvious. The lines rhyme in couplets. There are also
internal rhymes:

> Daith bech buide a úaim i n-úaim
> > ní súaill a vide la grein;
> fó for fluth sa mag már;
> > dag a dál, comol 'na chéir.

Here is Lehmann's imitative translation of the same:

> Bee, flying fast cup to cup,
> > sup in sun, hying from home;
> fair in flight toward the high heath,
> > nigh beneath come feast in comb.

Here is a poem of three-syllable lines:

> Int én bec
> ro léic feit
> do rinn guip
> >   glanbuide:
> fo-ceird faíd
> ós Loch Laíg,
> lon do chraíb
> >   charnbuide.

Here is Lehmann's imitative translation:

> Ousel sleek
> pipes so sweet
> from his beak
> >   broomyellow;
> song flung
> o'er Loch Laíg
> from tall tree
> >   bloomyellow.

In the Irish the first three lines, and also lines five, six, and seven, "rhyme" by consonance, and lines four and eight rhyme exactly. In the English the scheme is, with the exception of line seven, the same.

The strict metrical and rhyming rules these early poets made for themselves sometimes forced them to fill out a line with a parenthesis that makes little or no sense or to distort the word order in order to get a rhyme. On the whole, however, the tightness of the lines contributes to their vitality. In "The Blackbird by Belfast Loch" the rhyming words *glanbuidi* and *charnbuidi* mean "bright yellow" and "heap yellow." The latter presumably means a tree or bush (perhaps, as Murphy suggests, the gorse) bursting with yellow blossoms, rather like our forsythia in early spring. I have translated it "abundantly yellow," partly for the sounds in it—*b*, for instance, to resonate with *blackbird* and *branch;* partly because of the meter, which I intend to suggest blossoms bursting forth. In the Irish, however "heap yellow" is one word, *charnbuidi.* Its rhyme with *glanbuidi* above, together with the meter of this tight little compound, which is the final line of the poem, springs the imagination. We hear as well as see yellow blossoms bursting forth.

In "The Cry of the Garb" the first line has strong alliteration in *g* and assonance in *a* sounds: *Gáir na Gairbe glaídbinne.* Again, the compound *glaídbinne,* "musically roaring," makes this short line say more than its four words might suggest. The alliteration in *g* and the assonance in *a* sounds suggest the sound of rushing water, the noise that the Garb makes as it encounters the first waves of the sea. This line is reinforced by the end rhymes of the next three lines: *tuinne, aíbinne, brinne.* The soft sounds of these words suggest the shoals of fish swimming about the Garb.

In the evocation of the sights and sounds of nature these medieval Irish verses have much of their charm. Thus we have blossoming branches, the roaring of colliding waters, the belling of stags, billowing seas, trilling blackbirds, and dappled salmon. Other poems enchant because of the astounding beauty of faraway places; dazzling silver, gold, and jewels; fabulous food and drink; and lovely women. There are several haunting love stories, and stories of visionary voyages. A frequent theme is the sadness of growing old; men as well as women lament this process. The pathetic yet amusing tale of Suibne's madness produces poems of wildest fantasy. The homesickness of the self-exiled monks is another prevalent theme. The poems abound in the listings of the bounties of nature: grown and baby badgers, pigeons, woodcocks, herons, geese, foxes, wolves, rowanberries, strawberries, ashes, oaks, poplars, eggs, honey, mast, heathpease, mead, meadows, oceans, streams, and waterfalls.

The poems I have chosen for this collection are then remarkable for their sensuousness. They are pagan and wild, sweet and sad. My interpretations of them are in my translations. I have used the text of Gerard Murphy, and I owe much to his prose translation, his notes, and his glossary.[8] The occasional ellipses indicate passages in the original manuscripts that are obscure or corrupt.

8. See note 4.

monastic poems, ninth century

Pangur Ban

Pangur Ban, my cat, and I
practice each of us his art.
He puts his mind to hunting, while I
put mine to my particular craft.

I love better than fame to be
quiet with my book, intent
on gaining knowledge. Pangur Ban
doesn't care. He loves his childish art.

When the two of us are
(this story never wearies us)
alone in our house, we have our skills
to apply, our endless artful craft.

It's not unusual at times
of battling for a mouse to stick in his net.
As for me, what falls in my net
is a rule hard to understand.

He directs toward an encircling wall
his eye, which is perfect and bright. I
direct mine, which is clear but weak,
against knowledge's keen edge.

He rejoices with a quick pounce
when a mouse is caught in his sharp paw.
When I understand a difficult,
beloved problem, I too rejoice.

Though we are thus at any time,
neither hinders the other one.
Each of us loves his art,
rejoicing each of us alone.

He is himself master of
the work he does day by day.
At understanding clearly what
is difficult, I perform my task.

The Scribe in the Woods

A hedge of trees
hangs over me.
A blackbird sings
his lay, a message
I'll not conceal.
Above my book
marked with lines
carolling birds
sing to me.

From a fortress of hedge
in his gray cloak
a clarion cuckoo
calls. How good
God is to me!
Beautifully do
I write beneath
a hedge of trees.

The Bell

A bell of lovely sound
rings on a windy night.
I'd rather tryst with it
than with a wanton woman.

The Blackbird by Belfast Loch

The little bird has trilled
from the tip of its brilliant yellow bill.
It lets fall a note above
Belfast Loch—a blackbird
from a branch abundantly yellow.

The Blackbird Calling from the Willow

The bird that calls from the willow,
his beautiful little beak
sends forth a note that is clear,
a musical yellow bill
on a body sturdy and black.
Lively the tune,
the blackbird's voice.

King and Hermit

Gúaire: O hermit Marbán, why don't you sleep
    upon a bed? More often you'd sleep
    outside, where the tonsure ends,
    upon the ground of a grove of firs.

Marbán: I have a hut in the woods. My Lord
    alone is aware of it. On one side
    an ash, on the other a hazel like
    a tree by a rath, encloses it.

    Heather doorposts give support.
    Honeysuckle forms the lintel.
    The forest in its narrowness
    spills its nuts for fat swine.

    My hut is small, yet not small,
    a property with familiar paths.
    A woman in a blackbird's cloak
    from the gable sings a lovely song.

    The stags of Druim Rolach leap
    from its stream that sparkles through the plain.
    Ruddy Roigne can be seen
    and Mucruime and Móenmag.

    Little humble secluded abode,
    domain of a wood filled with paths.
    Will you go with me to see? My life
    has been happy even without you.

    Lengthy branches of
    a green yew tree.
    Marvelous the portent!
    Beautiful the place:
    the spreading green of an oak
    increases the augury.

There is an apple tree
with apples of fairyland
(enormous are the blessings)
and a goodly clustered crop
of hazel nuts from
brandishing green trees.

Choice wells are there
and waterfalls (fine
to drink) that spume forth
generously. Berries
of yew, bird cherry,
and privet, all are there.

All round about it
tame swine, goats,
young pigs, wild swine,
stately deer, does,
badger cubs, and badgers
grown have their lairs.

Gathered together in bands,
an enormous army at peace,
assembles at my house.
Before it arrives, foxes
come to the wood. It is
a truly lovely sight.

There come excellent feasts.
Preparation is swift.
Pure water . . . salmon
and trout. . . .

Crops of mountain ash.
Black sloes from
a dark blackthorn,
berries good to eat,
bare fruits of a bare . . .

There is a clutch of eggs,
honey, mast, and heathpease
(these are sent by God),
apples that are sweet,
cranberries, red,
whortleberries too.

There are beer and herbs,
a bed of strawberries,
red, delicious to taste.
Berries of yew are there,
hawthornes, and nut-
kernels also abound.

A cup of hazel mead,
excellent and served
with alacrity.
Acorns that are brown
and tangles of branches
with tasty blackberries.

When the summer comes,
a rich and lovely mantle
providing tasty savor:
wild marjoram,
earth-nuts, and *foltáin*.

The notes of wood pigeons
with iridescent breasts
(a movement that I love),
the song of a thrush, pleasant
and continuous,
sounds about my house.

Bees and beetles are there.
One hears a restrained hum,
an unsubstantial buzz.
Barnacle and brent geese,
shortly before Samain,
music wild and dark.

A nimble linnet, a brown
and agile wizard from
the hazel bough. There
are also woodpeckers
with plumage that is pied,
flocks and flocks of them.

Beautiful white birds,
herons and geese.
The sea sings to them.
Not sad is the song now sung
by the dun grouse from
the russet-colored heather.

Loudly lows the heifer
in summer time, when
the weather is at its brightest.
Neither bitter nor toilsome
is her life upon the rich
and delightfully fertile plain.

The voice of the wind against
a wood of branching trees.
On a gray and cloudy day
a river, tumbling, cascades,
the roar of it against
the rock, delicious music.

Lovely are the pines
making music for me—
all without hire.
Because of the blessing of Christ,
I am in no sadder state
at any time than you.

Though you delight in all
that you enjoy, wealth
exceeding all, I
am perfectly content
with what is given me
by my gentle Christ.

Without a moment of strife,
without the din of combat
that disturbs you so,
grateful to my Prince
who gives every good
here at home in my hut.

Gúaire: I'll give my mighty kingdom,
    Colmán's heritage,
    possession undisputed
    until my death, to live
    with you, my hermit Marbán.

monastic poems, tenth and eleventh centuries

I Am Eve

I am Eve, the wife of mighty Adam.
    It is I who angered Jesus then.
It is I who deprived my children of heaven. Rightly
    should I have gone upon the cross.

I had at my disposal a royal house.
    Awful the choice that ruined me.
Awful the punishment that withered me.
    Alas, not pure is my hand of that!

It is I who plucked the apple. It overcame
    my control. Women will never therefore
cease from behaving foolishly as long
    as they go on living in the light of day.

All Things to All Men

When I am among my elders,
I attest to the forbidding of games.
When I am among the wild,
they think me younger than they.

Manchán's Wish

I wish, O Son of the Living God,
    eternal and ancient King,
for a little hidden hut in the wild
    that it might be my home.

Water shallow and very gray,
    a clear pool nearby
to wash away my sins by grace
    of the Holy Spirit above.

A lovely wood neighboring it,
    enclosing on every side,
for nurture of birds of many notes,
    a shelter concealing them.

A southerly prospect to keep me warm,
    a little stream to cross
its glebe, bounteous choice soil
    nourishing every plant.

A few young men well disposed
    (their number we shall tell)
to be humble and obedient
    in their beseeching their King.

Four threes we need, also three fours
    (to meet every need)
and two sixes in the church as well
    for both the north and the south.

Six couples in addition to
    myself we need to have
to pray forever to the King
    who causes the sun to shine.

A delightful church, linen-bedecked,
 a dwelling for heaven's God,
brilliant lamps above the scriptures,
 which are white and pure.

One house to which to go for attention to
 the body without lust,
without boasting or contemplation of
 anything evil to do.

This is the husbandry I'd undertake,
 unconcealed my choice,
the true and fragrant leek, hens,
 dappled salmon, and bees,

Sufficiency of clothing for me
 from the King whose fame is fair,
to sit for a while in a certain place
 and there to pray to God.

poems about colum cille's (saint columba's) life

A Blue Eye Will Look Back

A blue eye will look back at Ireland,
never again to see its women and men.

It would be delightful, Son of my God,
    in marvelous voyages
to float across the flooding springs of the sea
    and come again to Ireland.

To Mag nÉolairg, by Benevenagh,
    across Lough Foyle,
where I might once again listen to
    the shrilling songs of swans.

Many flocks of seagulls would rejoice
    at the swiftness of our sailing
were the Red Dewey One to reach
    welcoming Port na Ferg.

Much did I sorrow when I was away from Ireland
    in the days that I had power,
making me melancholy and full of tears
    in an unfamiliar land.

Burdensome was the journey imposed upon me,
    King of Mysteries.
O would that I had never gone myself
    to the battle of Cúl Dreimne!

Happy am I for the fortune of Dímma's son
    in his sacrosanct cloister
where I might hear in Durrow in the west
    what would delight my mind.

The whisper of the wind in the elm making music for us.
    The startled, pleasant cry
of the dark and delightful blackbird when she has clapped
    both her wings for us.

Listening early in the morning to the stags
    that bell in Ross Grencha
and to the cuckoos calling from the forested land
    at the brink of summertime.

I have loved the lands of Ireland. (This
    a spontaneous utterance!)
To spend the night with Comgall, visit Cainnech,
    how lovely that would be!

Derry

This is why I love Derry:
it is so calm and bright because
it is filled with white angels from
one end to the other of it.

The Three Best Beloved Places

The three best beloved places I've left
    in all this peopled planet are
Durrow, Derry (lofty and haunted by
    angels), and then Tír Luigdech.

Did the sun and King of the angels allow it to me,
    I should choose for my burial place
Gartán much in preference to all
    other places in groups of three.

Weary My Hand with Writing

Weary my hand with writing.
Not thick is the tip of my quill.
Its delicate beak spews forth
a drink of beetle-black ink.

There springs a stream of wisdom
from my bright and beautiful work.
On the page it pours its drink
of green-leaved holly's ink.

I send my little pen
over lovely books to enrich
the possessions of men of art.
Weary my hand with writing.

The Old Woman of Beare

The ebbing of the tide has come to me
as to the sea. Old age has sallowed me.
Sad though I may be at that, still

happily does it approach its prey.
Buí am I, the old woman of Beare.
I used to wear a smock forever new.

Today, because of my humble estate, I've not
even a tattered cast-off smock to wear.
It is riches that you love, not mankind

you cherish. But we were different from you.
As long as we lived out our lives, it was
mankind we cherished and even loved.

Beloved were the men whose plains we rode upon.
Among those men well did we fare,
and afterward little had they to boast about.

Chariots, swift as the wind, and prize-winning steeds.
There's been a veritable flood of them.
A blessing upon the King who bestowed them.

With bitterness my body seeks to go
to a dwelling where it is recognized.
Let Christ come to take his deposit of grace.

Look at my arms. They're only skin and bones.
The art they used to practice was wonderful.
They used to embrace eminent sovereign kings.

When anyone sees my arms, all skin and bones,
it is not, I declare, worth my while
to lift them to embrace handsome youths.

The young girls rejoice when they come
to May Day. Grief better fits me. I'm not
miserable. I'm an ancient old crone.

I have no honied speech. No castrated rams
are slaughtered for my bridal. My hair is sparse and gray.
No cause for sorrow my wretched head veil.

I feel no grief for the white veil I wear
on my head. I had veils of every hue
upon my head when we drank delicious ale.

I'm jealous of no one except the plain
of Feimen. I have worn an old crone's
clothes. Feimen's crop is yellow still.

It is long since storms touched the cheeks of the Stone
of the Kings in Feimen, Rónán's dwelling place,
but they are neither wrinkled nor weathered by age.

Loud is the wave of the enormous sea.
Winter has begun its lifting of it.
Neither nobleman nor son of slave

do I expect to visit me today.
I know what they do. They row and row.
Cold the place the reeds of Áth Alma sleep.

Alas that I do not sail the sea of youth!
Many years of my beauty have disappeared.
My wantonness has been drained to the very dregs.

Alas, whatever haze there may be, I
must take my cloak even when the sun shines.
Age has come upon me. I recognize it.

The summer of youth I spent together with
its autumn. The first months of the winter of age
that overwhelm everyone have come to me.

In the beginning I spent my youth. That satisfies me.
Though small had been my leap beyond the wall,
the cloak would not still have been new.

Lovely the cloak of green my King has spread
over Drumain. Noble is the fuller of it,
spreading wool after its cover of rough cloth.

Indeed I am cold. Every acorn is doomed
to decay. After feasting with brilliant candles
how sad to find myself in the chapel's gloom.

I have had my time with kings, drinking mead
and wine. Now I drink water and whey,
sitting among withered old crones.

Let a cup of whey be
my ale. Let whatever vexes me
be God's will. Praying to you may I

.   .   .   .

I see on my cloak the stains of old age.
My sense deceives me. Gray is the hair that grows
through my skin. So does an ancient tree decay.

They've taken my right eye to sell for a land
that will forever be mine. My left eye too
they've taken to make my claim to that land secure.

There is the flood wave and also that
of the swift ebb. Whatever the flood wave brings
the ebb wave washes away from your hand.

I've known the flood wave and also the ebb
that comes after that. Because both of them
have come to me, I can recognize them.

May the flood wave not come to the silence of my cellar.
Although my retinue in the gloom is great,
a hand was laid upon every one of them.

Had Mary's son known that he would be beneath
my cellar's house pole! In no other way
have I been generous. I've said no to none.

It is altogether sad (man is the worst
of creatures) that we did not see the ebb
as we did the flood tide that came before.

It is fortunate for an island of the great sea,
for the flood comes to it after the ebb.
No flood after the ebb will come to me.

There is scarcely a dwelling today
that I can recognize, for what was then
in flood is now all in the wave of the ebb.

Créide's Lament for Dínertach

The arrows that murder sleep each hour
of the frigid night are lamenting love,
because of evenings spent with a man
who came from beside the land of Roigne.

Love for a man from another land
who surpassed his companions of equal age
has taken my brilliance away. No bloom
is left. It allows no sleep to me.

Sweeter than singing was his speech,
except for adoring Heaven's King.
A glorious flame, no boasting word,
his slender body a comfort to me.

As a child I was demure, and not
concerned with the wicked ways of lust.
Now that I've reached an unstable age,
a wantonness has tempted me.

I have all things good with Gúaire,
the king of Aidne, a cold land,
but my mind longs to go away
from my own to the land in Irlúachair.

In splendid Aidne, about the sides
of Cell Cholmáin, men sing of a flame
that comes from the south of Limerick
of graves. His name is Dínertach.

His terrible death, O Holy Christ,
torments my tender heart. These
are the arrows that murder sleep at each
hour of the long and frigid night.

Líadan Tells of Her Love for Cuirithir

Displeasing
is the deed I've done.
To what I've loved
I've caused chagrin.

It had been madness
not to do what he wished,
except for fear
of Heaven's King.

No disadvantage
to him was what he desired:
to avoid pain
and come to Paradise.

A little thing chagrined
Cuirithir in regard
to me. To him I was
as gentle as I could be.

I am Líadan.
I was in love with Cuirithir.
This is as true a word
as any ever told.

For a little while
I accompanied Cuirithir.
To be with me
was of profit to him.

Beside Cuirithir
woodland music would sing
to me in consonance with
the sound of the savage sea.

I'd have supposed
that nothing I'd proposed
would have caused chagrin
to Cuirithir in respect to me.

Hide it not:
he was the love of my heart,
even though I ought to love
everyone else as well.

A roaring of flame
has sundered my heart.
Without Cuirithir
it will never survive.

Poor Payment

I've heard he gives no horses for poems;
Instead he gives what he knows how:
A cow.

otherworld poems

Manannán Describes His Kingdom to Bran

Bran thinks it wonderful to go
in his coracle over the bright sea
while I drive my chariot from
afar over a blossoming plain.

What is a bright sea for Bran
in his prowed ship is a flowering
Plain of Delights for me as I drive
in my chariot with its two wheels.

Bran beholds many waves
breaking over the bright sea
while I see on the Plain of Feats
flawless flowers with crimson blooms.

In summer seahorses glisten over
the prospect that Bran can cast his eye.
Blossoms are bounteous with honey in the land
of Manannán, the son of Ler.

The sheen of the sea on which you sail,
the brilliance of ocean you voyage over
has poured forth yellow and green.
It has created solid earth.

Dappled salmon leap from the womb
of the silver sea that you behold.
They are lovely lambs and calves,
at peace, without mutual slaughter.

Though you'd see on the blossoming Plain of Delights
a single charioteer upon
its breast, there are many steeds
beside him that you do not see.

The enormous plain, the numerous host
are all aglow with brilliant hues.
A shining stream of silver, stairs
of gold create festival joy.

Shadowed by shrubbery, men
and gentle women play a game,
pleasant and delightful, without
wickedness or worldly sin.

Over ridges, the tip of a wood
your coracle has gone. Beneath
the prow of your little boat, there is
a beautiful forest bearing fruit.

There is a blossoming wood and fruit
fragrant from the vine, a wood
that does not decay, has no defect,
and has at its peak leaves of gold.

Since creatures were born, there's been a fort,
with neither age nor withering,
still fresh. We do not expect . . .
Original sin has touched us not.

Under evil auspice did
the serpent come to the father in
his house, corrupting him, and caused
a miserable ebbing of the tide.

He has ruined himself with gluttony and greed
and so destroyed his noble heirs.
With withered body he went to a prison
of pain, a place of infinite anguish.

The law of pride in this world
has caused belief in idols, of God
oblivion, diseases and age,
the death by deceit of the human soul.

Sublime deliverance shall come
from the King who created the firmament.
A holy law shall stir the seas.
He shall be man as well as God.

This form that you behold shall come
to your land. A journey is fated for me
to meet a woman in her homeland,
the country called Mag Line.

The man who speaks from the chariot
is Manannán, the son of Ler.
Among his children there shall be
a figure in bright body of clay.

Manannán, son of Ler,
shall be with Caíntigern,
be called to his son in the lovely world.
Fíachna will recognize him as his son.

He'll boast of pleasant frequentation
of every fairy home, and be
the darling of every land, fearless,
to tell mysteries to the world.

He'll be the shape of every beast
on land and on the azure sea,
in battle a dragon before the hosts,
The wolf of every enormous wood.

A stag with silver horns in a land
where chariots go, a dappled salmon
in a deep pool; he shall be
a seal and a beautiful white swan.

His reign shall last hundreds of years.
He shall hack down hills, a tomb
far distant, bloody a battlefield
in a swath made by chariot wheels.

Beside a warrior, together with kings
he shall be known as champion in battle
in a stronghold of land upon a height

. . . .

A noble one whom I shall know
among princes, a son of error,
Moininnán's son of Ler
shall be father and teacher.

His life shall be short: fifty years
in this world. A boulder slung by a hero
from the sea shall slay him
in course of battle at Old Labor.

He shall ask for a drink from Loch Ló
after his death . . . of blood.
The blessed host shall carry him
below the clouds to a joyous feast.

Steadily then let Bran row.
It is no distance to the land of women.
Before the sun sets he shall reach
Emnae of hospitality.

The Island with a Bridge of Glass

They rowed to an Island. It was not large
but there was a mighty fortress there.
On the fortress there was a fence
made of firm brass, a famous affair.

Around the fence there was a pool,
high above the waves of the sea,
more shining than all the tales.
Before it was a bridge of glass.

His fierce, brave, and blond young men
used to climb up, but fell
down to earth, a penalty
they had perpetually to pay.

A tender woman walked toward them.
Her throat was white, her nature free
of foolishness, her action fair,
her dress as radiant as the swan's.

Her lovely cloak was luminous
and had a border of ruddy gold.
It was beautiful, and on
her feet she wore sandals of silver.

She wore upon her breast a brooch.
Large and made of marvelous silver,
it was inlaid with woven gold
of most wonderful craftsmanship.

Like a sacred sanctuary in
the lower part of the bridge
was a well, shining as the waves,
covered with a handsome lid.

The lovely one poured liquor out
before them; delicious it was, but
she offered no one a drink of it.
Her behavior was astonishing.

In a loud voice Germán spoke
appropriate words to her: "Amazed
are we that you have not thought to serve
any of the lovely liquor you poured."

She left them and closed the noble fort.
The brazen net that hung from the door,
manifesting indisputable might,
sounded pleasant harmonious song.

Her melodious chorus lulled them to sleep,
for that was what had been ordained.
On the following morning she came to them,
a woman completely unashamed.

So they stayed just as they were
until the third day arrived.
The noble woman's music played,
but no banqueting hall appeared.

She took them to a huge house
above the swift and savage sea.
There an excellent meal was served
together with delicious drink.

The woman, behaving modestly,
spoke wonderful names and honored them
by calling each and every one
by his own particular name.

When she had been begged to satisfy
their leader's lustful desire,
she replied that she had no knowledge
at all of worldly wickedness.

"Not properly do you speak. You have
no share of sanctity. You renounce
proper principles. Ask
the island's secret. I'll tell it to you."

When in the morning they awoke
in the shell of their boat, they knew
nothing at all about whence
the lovely island had disappeared.

Fair Lady, Will You Go with Me?

Fair Lady, will you go with me
to a marvelous land where there are stars?
Hair is the color of primroses there,
and all the flesh is white as snow.

There, there is no "mine" or "yours."
Teeth are white and brows are black.
All our hosts delight the eye.
Every cheek of foxglove hue.

Purple the surface of every plain.
A blackbird's egg enchants the eye.
Though pleasant the prospect of Ireland's plain,
it's desolate beside the Great Plain.

Though you consider Ireland's beer
intoxicating, more so is theirs,
The land I mention is marvelous.
The young do not die before the old.

The earth is watered by sweet streams.
We drink the best of mead and wine.
Perfect are the people there.
Conception has no guilt or sin.

We see every one about,
and no one sees us, because
the darkness caused by Adam's sin
prevents them from counting us.

If you come to my stalwart folk,
you'll wear a crown of gold upon
your head and have with me ale,
milk, fresh pork, and wine to drink.

Lóeg's Description to Cú Chulainn of Labraid's Home in Mag Mell

I came on my splendid venture
to a wondrous establishment,
to a populous hill and found
Labraid of the long hair.

He was seated upon the hill.
Thousands of weapons there.
His hair was beautifully blond,
caught with a clasp of gold.

Then he recognized me
from his purple five-fold cloak.
He said, "Will you go with me
to the house of Fáilbe Find?"

There are two kings there,
Fáilbe Find and Labraid.
Each has a following
of one hundred fifty men.

They are all housed there.
Fifty beds on the right,
fifty beds on the left.
Fifty couches too.

A border of blood-red beds.
Their posts are white and crowned
with gold. The candle there
is a glowing precious stone.

Where the sun sinks in the west
there is a stud of horses,
gray with rainbow manes,
and another stud, red-brown.

To the east there stand three trees
of crimson glass. From them
sleek and insistent birds
call to the folk from the fort.

In front there is a tree.
A joy to sing with it!
The sun shines like gold
upon that silver tree.

Sixty trees are there.
Their branches almost meet.
They fill three hundred men
with abundant huskless nuts.

In that fairy house
there is a well that holds
thrice fifty rainbow cloaks,
each with a clasp of gold.

A vat of merry mead
is served to all the house.
It flows unceasingly
and is forever full.

There is a maid in the house
surpassing Ireland's women.
Her golden hair blows free.
She is lovely and very skilled.

Her talk with everyone
is enchantingly beautiful.
Everyone's heart is breaking
with love and longing for her.

Then the maiden spoke:
"Whose servant is this boy?
If servant of the man
from Muirtheimne, come close."

Forward I slowly stepped,
shy at the honor done me.
"Will Dechtere's noble
only son step forth?"

Alas that he hadn't gone,
when all were seeking him,
so as to see what the house
that I have seen is like.

Were all of Ireland mine
and bright Brega too,
I'd give it all to dwell
in the house to which I came.

poems
attributed
to
mad
suibne

My Little Chapel

Mad Suibne:

My little chapel in Túaim Inbir—
a palace could not be pleasanter—
with the orderly stars of the firmament
together with its sun and moon.

Gobbán it was who built it
so that its story could be told.
My beloved God from Heaven
was the thatcher who roofed it over.

A house in which it never rains.
A shelter where spears are never feared.
There is no wattling surrounding it.
It is as radiant as a garden.

The Cry of the Garb

Suibne: The cry of the musically roaring Garb
    sounding against the first wave
    of the sea! Large and beautiful
    schools of fish swim in its breast.

My patient watch is nothing to me:
my seeing the tides that flood the banks,
the surging torrent of the great Garb
and the water of the sea thrusting it back.

I like to see how the two of them struggle,
the flood with the cold ebb tide.
They happen each in proper succession,
flowing forever up and down.

I hear harmonious music in
the Garb in the time of its winter's brilliance.
I sleep to the sound of boisterous mirth
on a very frigid and icy night.

Melodious birds of the Garb's shore,
musically sweet their constant calls!
A lonely longing comes over me
to hear their calling out the hours.

I love to hear the warbling of blackbirds
and also to listen to the Mass.
Time passes quickly for me
reposing above Durad Faithlenn.

I sleep to their melodies upon
mountain peaks and tops of trees.
The melodies I hear are music
to my very heart and soul.

The singing of pure psalms at the point
of Ros Bruic, impermanently named;
the roar of the belling brown stag
from the mountain side of chilly Erc;

A frigid sleep through an entire night
as I listen to the billowing sea;
the loud echoing calls of birds
from the forest of Fid Cuille;

The breath of wintry wind; the sound
of storm beneath an oak tree;
the cold sheets of ice roar,
breaking up at the cry of the Garb.

It is difficult to hear
the canonical hours at which
loud bells ring because of the sound
of Inber Dubglaise and the cry of the Garb.

The water of the sounding sea
flowing westward around the approach
to Airbre—it makes the time pass
to listen at rest to the cry of the Garb.

Variegated Druim Lethet
has acorns that are brown on its oak.
Its echo is a miracle which
answers me with the cry of the Garb.

Though much be told of the waterfalls
at Máige, Dubthaige, Assaroe,
where the salmon run, the voice
of the Garb is more musical by far.

Benn Boirche, Benn Bógaine,
and silent Glenn Bolcáin; many
an evening, many a night have I
come from them to the Garb's cry.

Tonn Túaige and Tonn Rudraige:
time passes more quickly for me when I
hear the cry of the Garb than when
I linger beside their sounding waves.

How musical the high cascade
of the powerful prophesied watercourse!
The angelic stream of Tacarda,
what cascade is clearer in cry?

O Mo Ling, beloved of me,
I come to you to play out the end
of my game. May you defend me
against hell whose cry is cruel!

Suibne and Éorann

Suibne: You enjoy sleep, glorious Éorann,
    pledged to a bed with your lover, Gúaire.
    It is not that way here with me.
    I have been restless for a long time.

    Lightly, lovely Éorann,
    did you make that pleasant utterance,
    that you'd not live were you to be parted
    from Suibne for a single day.

    Today it can soon be seen that you
    little value your old friend.
    You are warm on the down of a bed.
    I am cold without till dawn.

Éorann: Welcome to you, brilliant madman;
    you are the dearest of all men.
    Although I sleep well, I waste
    away since I learned that you were mad.

Suibne: More dear to you is the king's son
    who takes you to the happy feast.
    He is the suitor whom you prefer.
    You do not seek your old friend.

Éorann: Though the king's son takes me
    to happy feastings, I should prefer
    to spend the night in a hollow tree
    with you, O husband, if only I could.

Suibne: Better to give affection and love
    to the husband who has you as his wife
    than to a famished, terrifying,
    uncouth, and naked man.

Éorann: Had I the choice of all the men
　　of Scotland and Ireland given me,
　　I should choose to live with you,
　　blamelessly, on water and cress.

Suibne: No path for a beloved lady is that
　　of Suibne, who is on the track
　　of trouble. My beds at Ard Abla
　　are cold. Cold houses are common there.

Éorann: It saddens me, my laboring madman,
　　that you should be ugly and distressed.
　　It grieves me that your skin is pale,
　　that thorns and briars tear at your flesh.

Suibne: I speak not to find fault with you,
　　sensitive, radiant, gentle lady:
　　Christ, the son of Mary, it is
　　who has enslaved me in this distress.

Éorann: If only we could be together
　　and feathers cover over our bodies
　　and I roam through light and dark
　　with you every day and night!

Suibne: I have spent a night in sounding Boirche.
　　I have traveled to lovely Túag Inbir.
　　I have roamed all over Ireland and seen
　　Suánach's grandson's monastery.

Suibne in the Woods

Antlered, belling one,
you of the musical roar,
lovely is the sound
that you make in the glen.

A longing for my home
overtook my soul—
for the grass in the plain and for
the fawns upon the moors.

Oak of spreading leaves,
taller than any tree.
the delicate little hazel,
a coffer for its nuts.

Alder, you are not
malevolent. You gleam
splendidly, are not
prickly where you are.

Blackthorn, dark bearer
of sloes. Watercress,
green at the top, from the edge
of a blackbird's well.

Little one of the path,
tastier than any herb,
greener than green the plant
on which the strawberry grows.

Apple tree, all men
shake you forcefully.
Rowanberry tree,
your blossom is beautiful.

Briar that grows in ridges,
you don't play fair. You won't
stop scratching me until
you've had your fill of blood.

Yew tree, you are seen
in churchyards. Ivy,
you are frequently found
in a deep and dark wood.

Holly, you shelter one,
protection against the wind.
Ash tree, pernicious one,
a weapon for a warrior.

Birch, blessed and smooth,
musical and proud,
lovely every branch
entangled at your top.

The poplar, its quivering
I hear in good time.
Its quickly trembling leaves
put me in mind of a raid.

What I dislike in woods
(I keep it not from all):
an infertile, leafing oak
swaying forever more.

Ill omened was my affront
to the honor of Rónán Finn:
his monastery bells
and miracles did me harm.

Ill omened was the raiment
I got from worthy Congal—
his brightly adorned tunic,
lovely, with fringes of gold.

Every man in that army,
brave and swift, called out,
"Don't let the man in that tunic
get away through the narrow copse.

Slaughter, slay, and kill!
Take the chance you've got.
Dreadful though the deed,
put him on spike and spear."

The horsemen chase me over
rounded Mag Coba,
but no cast of their spears
pierces me through my back.

As I sped over ivied trees
(I'll not conceal it, warrior),
the well-cast dart would succeed,
swifter than the wind.

Doe of delicate shins,
I have control of you.
I ride upon your back
from one peak to another.

From Carn Cornáin I ride
to the peak of Slíab Níad.
From the peak of Slíad Níad
I come to the Galtee Mountains.

From the Galtee Mountains where
men assemble I ride
to Lorc's Carn Liffe. At evening
I reach Gort's Binbulbin.

The night before Congal's
battle was happy for me.
I did not wander yet
over the mountain peaks.

Glenn Bolcáin is my home,
for I have made it my own.
Often at night I practiced
strenuous running to peaks.

Did I wander alone
over the hills of the world,
I should choose a single hut
in the Glenn of mighty Bolcáin.

Good its water, pure
and blue, its sharp wind,
its green watercress.
Better its water parsnip.

Good its ivy-clad tree.
Good its brilliant willow.
Good its yew, better
its melodious birch.

Loingsechán, if you
were in any fashion
nightly to talk to me,
I might not wait for you.

I'd not have awaited your talk
were it not for your wounding news:
the deaths of my father and mother,
brother, children, and wife.

Your coming to talk to me
would please me no more. Before
dawn I'd seek out
the mountains of Benna Boirche.

By means of the miller's mill
you used to grind for the folk,
wretched weary one,
Loingsechán the quick.

Old woman of the mill,
why do you take advantage
of me? I hear your abuse
as you rest on the mountain peak.

Pointy-headed hag,
will you ride a horse?
"I would steeple-head,
if no one could see me.

Suibne, if I do,
lucky be my leap."
If you come, you hag,
may you dismount insane.

"Not proper is what you say,
son of curly Colmán;
won't I ride the better,
if I don't fall off my horse?"

Proper is what I say,
you demented old hag.
A devil destroys you.
You have ruined yourself.

"Slender, noble madman,
does my following you
over mountain peaks
not please you more with my arts?"

I'd be afraid to leave
an ivy thrusting through
a twisted tree, although
I sat upon its peak.

I flee from the larks at a rush,
strong and impetuous.
I leap over the stalks
that grow on mountaintops.

When the noble wood pigeon
rises up for me,
I'm quick to overtake,
for my feathers have grown.

When the idiotic
woodcock rises for me,
I think the blackbird's call
of alarm my enemy.

Whenever, leaping, I leapt
to the ground, I'd discover down there
the little red fox
busily gnawing bones.

More quickly he'd better me
than any hound among
the ivy-cloaked trees.
I'd leap to the mountain peak.

Cunning little foxes
approach and run from me.
I flee at the howling of wolves
for their ferocity.

Running fiercely, they tried
to overtake me, but I
fled before those wolves
to the very mountain peaks.

My sin has followed me
no matter where I go.
My lamentations prove
that I'm a foldless sheep.

Soundly I sleep in
Lugaid's monastery.
More pleasant in Congal's time
was Line's crowded fair.

Stars of frost will come
to cover every pond.
I am a sorry vagrant
exposed to it on the peaks.

The heron's call is heard
in cold Glenelly.
Swiftly a flock of birds
flies to me and away.

I care not for lovers' talk,
the words of women and men.
A blackbird's warbling is
more musical to me.

I care not for the trumpets
that sound at dawn. The cry
of badgers on mountain peaks
is more musical to me.

I care not for the horns
which I anxiously hear. The belling
of a forty-antlered stag
is more musical to me.

From glen to glen a team
for a plough can be found:
every stag that lies
upon the mountain peaks.

Though many my stags from glen
to glen, seldom does
a farmer fasten a yoke
upon their antlered horns.

The stag of Slieve Phelim,
the fierce stag of the Fews,
the Duhallow, and Orrery,
the stag of Lough Leane,

The stags of Island Magee,
of Laire, of Moylinny
of cloaks, of Cooley, Cunghill,
and Burren of double peaks.

O mother of this herd,
your coat has become gray.
Every stag of yours
has forty antlers now.

Enough of your head is gray
to make a little cloak.
On every fawn an antler,
an antler on every fawn.

O stag that calls for me
across the mountain glen,
the tips of your antlers would be
a lovely lookout place.

I am the vagrant Suibne.
Quickly I cross a glen.
Suibne is no name for me.
I am the Antler Man.

The best wells I've found
are those of populous Layd,
the most delicious and cool,
the spring of Dún Máil.

Many my wanderings,
scanty my clothing today.
I keep my watch upon
the tops of mountain peaks.

Tall ruddy bracken,
your cloak's become crimson,
the forkings of your tops
no bed for an outcast man.

Beside Taídiu in the south
my final rest will be.
At Mo Ling's monastery
I shall fall by an antler peak.

The curse of Rónán Finn
has made me your companion,
antlered, belling stag,
you of melodious cry.

Suibne in the Snow

Greatly do I grieve tonight.
The fierce wind has pierced my flesh.
Wounded my feet and pale my cheek.
Great God, I have good cause.

I was in the Mourne Mountains last night.
In cold Aughty I was pelted by rain.
Tonight all my flesh has been rent
in the fork of a tree in brilliant Gáille.

Many stalwart assaults have I
endured since feathers grew on my flesh.
As each day and night go by,
the more the suffering that I endure.

Cruel frost has tortured me;
in the Kerry Stacks, the blinding snow.
Far from the heather of Glenn Bolcáin
tonight the wind has wounded me.

Restlessly I wander from
place to place, unhappily insane.
From Moylinny to Mag Lí
and then to the rough Liffcy Vale.

I cross Segan upon the Fews.
In my rush I reach Rathmore.
Through Mag nAí and Plains of Boyle
I reach the hill of Crúachán

From the mountains of Knockmealdown
I reach the river in lovely Gáille.
From the Gáille River I make my way
east to the melodious Slieve Brey.

Dreary my days without a house.
Good Christ, it is a wretched life,
forever green cress for food, for drink
cold water from a frozen stream!

Tumbling down from withered boughs,
going through gorse, avoiding men,
with wolves for company; racing
a red stag over the moor.

To spend the night featherless
at the top of a thick bushy tree in a wood,
hearing no human voice or speech,
Son of God, causes me grief.

Wild, I rush to a mountain peak;
few have been more agile than I.
I have lost all my comeliness.
Son of God, it causes me grief.

poems from the finn cycle

Cáel Praises Créide's House

Worried, I travel on Friday,
though I am a proper guest,
to Créide's house which lies
northeast of the mountain's face.

I am destined to go there
to Créide in the Paps Mountains
to spend four days and half
a week in trouble there.

Delightful is her house
in men, women, boys,
druids, butler, musicians,
the keeper of the door,

graceful equerry,
carver of meat to share.
Lovely golden-haired
Créide rules them all.

It will be pleasant for me
in her house, both for bed
and its down. If Créide wishes,
my journey will have been fine.

Her black shawl was washed
in berry juice in a bowl.
No lees in her glass vat.
Lovely goblets and cups.

Her color as fresh as lime.
A quilt against the rushes.
Silk beneath her cloak
of blue. Red-gold the bangle

between her and her gleaming
drinking horn. Her bower
is silver and gold with thatch
of brown and crimson feathers.

The two doorposts are green;
Lovely the leaves of the door.
The beam that makes her lintel
is of pure silver, they say.

At your left is Créide's chair,
incredibly beautiful;
at the foot of her lovely bed
a clasp of Alpine gold.

The poem's glowing bed
above the chair was made
of gold and precious stone
by Tuile in the east.

At the right another bed,
wrought of silver and gold.
It has an awning that glows
like hyacinth and rods of bronze.

The members of her house—
happily were they born—
their cloaks not gray or worn,
their hair curly and blond.

Wounded men spouting
blood would sleep to the songs
of fairy birds that sing
above her bower's eaves.

If I am to thank Créide,
for whom the cuckoo calls,
her poems shall survive,
if only she pays my reward.

If Cairbre's daughter wills,
she will not ignore me long
but will say to me here,
"Your journey is welcome indeed."

There are a hundred feet
in Créide's house from one
end to the other of it.
And fifty feet to the door.

Her wattling and thatch are made
from feathers of blue and yellow
birds; the rail beside the well,
of carbuncle and glass.

Around the bed four pillars
of patterned silver and gold.
A gem of glass crowns
each pillar pleasantly.

A princely enameled vat
catches the juice of malt;
an apple tree above,
abundant in heavy fruit.

When Créide's goblet is full
of mead from that vat,
four apples fall at once
into the goblet she holds.

The master of all, the flood
and the ebb, has set Créide
from Tulcha Trí mBenn beyond
Ireland's women by the cast

of a spear. No curly cattle
have I brought but a poem
of temperate tone to Créide
to please her with my arrival.

Créide's Lament for Cáel

The harbor roars over
the rushing stream of Reenverc.
The wave that beats the shore
bewails the drowning of

the warrior from Loch Dá Chonn.
A heron cries in the marsh.
She cannot save her young.
A parti-colored fox

is tracking them. Sad
the call of the thrush in Drumkeen.
Equally sad is the cry
of the blackbird in Leiter Laíg.

Sad is the sound of the stag
in Drumlesh. Dead is the doe
of Druim Sílenn. The stag
roars because she is gone.

Tragic the death of the warrior
who used to lie with me.
That the son of the woman from
Daire Dá Dos should have

a cross above his head!
Tragic that Cáel should be
dead at my side, that a wave
should have drowned his comely body.

His beauty made me wild.
Sad the cry of the wave
that strikes against the beach.
It has drowned a prince.

Tragic that Cáel went near.
Sad is the sound of the wave
on the northern shore as it roils
around an enormous rock,

bewailing Cáel dead.
Sad the strife of the wave
against the southern shore.
My life has reached its end.

My appearance has suffered too.
Strange is the music of
the wave of Tulach Léis.
My riches are nothing to me.

Since Crimthan's son has drowned,
there's no one else I can love.
Chieftains fell by his hand.
His shield never complained.

Description of Winter

The winter is frigid. The wind has risen.
The stark-savage stag rises up.
Not warm the massive mountain tonight,
even though the swift stag bells.

The Slievecarran of the assemblies' stag does not
put his flank to the ground. The stag
of the head of Aughty hears
as well the howling music of wolves.

I, Caílte, and Díarmait, whose hair was brown,
and Oscar, sharp and bright, used too
to listen to the music of wolves
at the close of an exceptionally cold night.

Well indeed does the brown stag sleep.
He presses his pelt to Corran's earth
as though beneath the water of Tuns
at the close of an exceptionally cold night.

Today I am aged and old. There are few
of men I recognize. Once
I brandished bravely a keen spear
on a morning of exceptionally cold ice.

I thank the King of Heaven, Son
of Virgin Mary. Often did I
quiet armies, though I am
tonight as cold as winter's ice.

May Day

May Day, a pretty prospect.
The year's perfection of season.
Blackbirds trill at the full.
The sun shines sparingly.

The strenuous cuckoo calls.
Welcome to perfect summer.
It stills the bitterness
of blizzards breaking branches.

Summer shrinks the stream.
Swift steeds seek water.
The high heather spreads.
Foliage flourishes fair.

The bud of the hawthorn blooms.
Smoothly the ocean runs.
Summer sends it to sleep.
Blossom blankets the earth.

Bees bear on their feet
bundles of blossoms culled.
The mountain tempts away
cattle with its abundance.

The forest plays a song
providing perfect peace.
From dwellings dust is blown
and haze from brimming lakes.

The vigorous corncrake calls.
The cascade, steep and clear,
sings for joy at the water
warmed. The reeds are rustling.

Swallows swoop above.
Strength of music surrounds
the hill. The rich and mellow
fruit flourishes now.

The strenuous cuckoo calls.
The trout leaps. Strong is the quick warrior's . . .

·   ·   ·   ·   ·   ·   ·   ·   ·   ·   ·   ·   ·   ·

·   ·   ·   ·   ·   ·   ·   ·   ·   ·   ·   ·   ·   ·

The vigor of men does thrive.
Perfect the green slopes,
and every woodland expanse,
and all the spreading plain.

The season is a delight.
Gone is winter's wind.
The forest gleams, water
is fecund, summer a joy.

A flock of birds settles
where a woman walks.
There is a gurgling in green fields
where sparkling rivers run.

Arduous riding of horses;
the host arranged around.
The pond is bounteous,
turning the iris to gold.

The timorous man fears noise.
The brave man sings with heart.
Rightly does he sing forth,
"May Day, a pretty prospect!"

These are my tidings to you.
The stag bellows; winter
storms; summer is gone.

The wind is piercing and cold.
The sun is low in the sky.
Its circuit is very brief.
The sea runs loud and high.

The bracken has turned bright red.
Concealed its confirmation.
The call of the barnacle goose
is familiar now to all of us.

Cold has caught the wings
of birds. It's the time of ice.
These are my tidings to you.

Gráinne Speaks of Díarmait

There is a man
at whom I'd gladly gaze.
To him I'd give the bright world,
all of it, all of it, even though
the bargain would be far from fair.

These hands are withered, these deeds
foregone. The flood tide has gone,
the ebb tide has come. It has
destroyed this vigor of mine.

I thank the Creator that I
have had beneficent joy.
Long my wretched life.
I was beautiful once.

In assembly I was fair.
I have enjoyed women
of wantonness. Stalwart,
I leave. My spring has gone.

These little fragments you break
for a famished wretch: a piece
on a stone, a piece on a bone,
a piece on this withered hand.

Once I Had Golden Curls

Once I had golden curls.
Now my crown sprouts only
a short crop of hoary hair.

I'd prefer to have raven locks
upon my head rather than
this scanty crop of hoary hair.

Wooing is not for me. I wile
no women. Tonight my hair is hoar.
I'll never be as once I was.

Notes

Pangur Ban

This poem was discovered with other Irish poems, together with a commentary on Vergil, examples of Greek paradigms, and astronomical notes, in a ninth-century manuscript at the Monastery of Saint Paul, Unterdrauberg, Carinthia (southern Austria). It is evidence of the pilgrimages Irish monks liked to make and a fine example of how their classical learning paralleled their ability to write charming verse in the vernacular. *Pangur* is an old spelling of the Welsh *pannwr*, "a fuller." *Ban* means "white." Perhaps Pangur was a Welsh cat.

The Scribe in the Woods

These verses appear in the lower margins of a copy of Priscian's treatise on Latin grammar done by Irish scribes in the first half of the ninth century.

The Bell, The Blackbird by Belfast Loch, The Blackbird Calling from the Willow

These are fragments of stanzas cited to illustrate rules of meter. They appear to be in ninth-century Irish.

King and Hermit

A dialogue between Gúaire, king of Connacht (died A.D. 663 or 666), and his half brother, Marbán, a hermit. The poem is ninth century. *Foltain* is an unidentified plant. Samain is November 1, a pagan holiday.

I Am Eve

The poem is in Middle Irish and belongs probably to the tenth or eleventh century.

All Things to All Men

In three manuscripts this quatrain appears in a Middle Irish commentary on the Old Irish Félire (festology) written by Óengus Céile Dé about A.D. 800. It was a comment on the entry for the saint Mo Ling's feast day, June 17. Mo Ling, of Saint Mullins, county Carlow, to whom this quatrain is attributed, died ca. A.D. 697.

Manchán's Wish

Saint Manchán of Líath died in A.D. 665. The poem is either ninth or early tenth century.

A Blue Eye Will Look Back, An Exile's Dream, Derry, The Three Best Beloved Places, Weary My Hand with Writing

These poems are attributed to Colum Cille, a saint who died in A.D. 597. He was born in Gartan, county Donegal, in the district formerly known as Tír Luigdech. Derry and Durrow were monasteries founded by him. His exile to Scotland was self-imposed (see introduction). The poems date to the eleventh century.

An Exile's Dream

Mag nÉolairg: Probably a poetic name for the part of Lough Foyle near Derry.

Benevenagh: A mountian over Loch Foyle.

Lough Foyle: County Derry.

Red Dewey One: Apparently the name of Colum's ship.

Port na Ferg: Apparently on Lough Foyle.

Cúl Dreimne: A place between Drumcliff and the town of Sligo. Colum Cille fought
a battle there in A.D. 561.

Dímma's son: Colum's friend Cormac uaLíatháin, abbot of Durrow, near Tullamore,
county Offaly.

Ross Grencha: The district in which Durrow was located.

Comgall: Comgall of Bangor (county Down) died in A.D. 602. A friend of Colum.

Cainnech: Abbot of Aghaboe (county Leix). Also a friend of Colum. The three friends
(see above), together with Brendan of Clonfest, county Galway, visited Colum in
Scotland.

The Three Best Beloved Places

This quatrain is attributed to Colum Cille, although its language is that of the
twelfth rather than the sixth century. For Derry, Durrow, and Tír Luigdech, see
preceding notes.

Weary My Hand with Writing

The poem belongs to the Late Middle Irish period, late eleventh or twelfth century.

The Old Woman of Beare

The manuscripts (around A.D. 800) attribute this poem to Buí, the Old Woman of
Beare. She was originally a mythological figure, ancestress of races, builder of mountains
and cairns. Eighth- or ninth-century writers, however, saw her as a very old human
being who had outlived her friends and lovers and took the veil from Saint Cuimíne.
The poem was composed in the eighth or ninth century. Cuimíne was probably the
Kerry saint who lived A.D. 592–662. Beare is a peninsula of southwest county Cork.
Feimen is a plain in county Tipperary. "Feimen's crop is yellow still": the Old Irish
word *barr* means both "crop" and "hair." Rónán: the saint who died in A.D. 664. Áth
Alma is an unidentified place. Drumain is also an unidentified place.

Créide's Lament for Dínertach

Créide was the daughter of Gúaire of Aidne. Gúaire was king of Aidne (county Galway).
In A.D. 649 he, together with his Munster allies, was defeated in the battle of Carn
Conaill by Díarmait, the king of Ireland. Dínertach of the Ui Fidgente (the people of
county Limerick), for whom Gúaire's daughter made this lament, was probably one
of Gúaire's Munster allies. Irlúachair is northeast county Kerry with adjoining parts of

counties Cork and Limerick. Cell Cholmáin is a monastery in Aidne. The poem dates
to about A.D. 800.

Líadan Tells of Her Love for Cuirithir

Líadan is said to have been a poet of the early seventh century. Her story is presented
in ninth-century Irish in two sixteenth-century manuscripts. The prose account,
together with the poetry it contains, seems to say that Líadan had promised to marry
Cuirithir but took the veil instead. Cuirithir then became a monk. Líadan followed him
to his monastic cell among the Déisi, a people inhabiting modern county Waterford.
Cuirithir then sailed across the sea from her, and she died praying upon the stone on
which he used to pray among the Déisi.

Poor Payment

The poem is ninth century. It is cited as an example of "slap-on-the-buttocks" meter.

Manannán Describes His Kingdom to Bran

This is an eighth-century poem preserved in a sixteenth-century manuscript, *The
Voyage of Bran*. The prose preceding these stanzas tells us that when Bran had been at
sea for two days and two nights, he saw a man approaching him over the sea in a
chariot. That man declared that he was Manannán, the son of Ler, that it was destined
for him to come to Ireland after long periods of time, and that a son should be born
to him called Mongán the son of Fíachna. He then sang these stanzas.

Manannán was the god of the sea. He was the son of Ler, an older god of the sea.
Bran was a prehistoric legendary hero of the eighth-century tale *The Voyage of Bran*.
Mongán, son of Fíachna, was ruler of an east Ulster kingdom; he died ca. A.D. 625. Mag
Line is Moylinney, county Antrim. Caíntigern is the wife of Fíachna and mother of
Mongán. Moininnán is a form of Manannán. Old Labor and Loch Ló are unidentified
places. Emnae is a place in the otherworld.

The Island with a Bridge of Glass

The rowers were the crews of two ships commanded by Máel Dúin and his companions
Germán and Díurán Leccard. This poem comes from a version of "The Voyage of
Máel Dúin's Currach," which tells of a voyage made in early Christian times during
which the companions visited many fabulous islands. The "His" in the third stanza
refers to Máel Dúin. The poem dates to about A.D. 920.

Fair Lady, Will You Go with Me?

The prose that precedes this poem says that the year before Midir came to Echaid he had
been wooing Étain but could not win her. The name he gave her was Bé Find (Fair Lady).
Earlier it was told how Midir had come from the underworld to play chess with Echaid,
king of Tara. Midir asked that as a prize for victory in the third chess game he be allowed
to embrace and kiss Étain, Echaid's wife. The poem dates to the late ninth century.

Lóeg's Description to Cú Chulainn of Labraid's Home in Mag Mell

This poem is taken from "The Wasting Sickness of Cú Chulainn," which tells how Cú Chulainn, the great pagan hero, was thrown into a wasting sickness and then invited to visit Mag Mell (the Plain of Delights) to enjoy the love of Fann, wife of Manannán, and to assist her friend Labraid in battle. Before Cú Chulainn went to Mag Mell himself, he sent his charioteer, Lóeg, to find out what it was like. In this poem, then, Lóeg describes Labraid's home. Labraid and Fáilbe Find were kings in the otherworld. Muirtheimne was a district including a large part of county Louth. Dechtere is the mother of Cú Chulainn. Brega is a place in county Meath and the south of county Dublin. The poem dates to the late eleventh century.

My Little Chapel

A poem of about A.D. 800, attributed to Mad Suibne who was said to have lost his reason at the battle of Mag Rath (A.D. 639) in northern Ireland, and who afterward lived in the wilderness. The saint Mo Ling befriended him at the end of his life. Gobbán was a mythical magical builder.

The Cry of the Garb

This poem dates to about A.D. 1150 and is attributed to Mad Suibne.

Garb (Rough) is apparently the name given to the tidal waves of the river Barrow, which ran next to Mo Ling's monastery (county Carlow).

Durad Faithlenn: A place in the Garb district.

Ros Bruic: An old name for Mo Ling's monastery.

Erc: An unidentified place.

Fid Cuille (the Wood of Cuilenn): A place in the Garb district.

Inber Dubglaise: An estuary of the Glynn River, south county Carlow.

Airbre: A district in county Wexford.

Druim Lethet: An unidentified place, probably in county Carlow.

Máige: The Maigue River.

Ess Dubthaige: An unidentified waterfall.

Ess Assaroe: Also a waterfall.

Benn Boirche: A peak of the Mourne Mountains.

Benn Bógaine: A mountain somewhere in northern Ireland.

Glenn Bolcáin: A glen in the north of Ireland frequented by Suibne.

Tonn Túaige (Wave of Túag): The Tuns in the mouth of the river Brann.

Tonn Rudraige (Wave of Rudraige): In Dundrum Bay, county Down.

Tacarda: A stream running from the holy well at Mo Ling's monastery.

"Whose cry is cruel": Literally "whose cry is rough"—that is, "garb."

Suibne and Éorann

This poem and the two that follow are found in the prose narrative of a late twelfth-century version of *Builne Suibne* (The Madness of Suibne).

Éorann had formerly been Suibne's wife but was now married to Gúaire. One day while Gúaire was out hunting, Suibne came to Éorann's hut, and the following verse dialogue ensued.

Ard Abla: Perhaps Lisardowlin near the town of Longford.

Boirche: See note to "The Cry of the Garb."

Túag Inbir: An estuary of the Bann on the coast of county Derry.

Suánach's Grandson's monastery (Cell Uí Súanaig): Probably Rahen, a place near Tullamore, county Offaly. This and the two preceding place names are given in the Old Irish forms for the sake of the meter.

Suibne in the Woods

Suibne had been lured home by his foster brother, Loingsechán, the owner of a mill, who shocked him out of his madness by dishonestly telling him of the deaths of all his family. The old woman of the mill, who had been left in charge of Suibne during his recovery, asked Suibne to tell her of his life in the wilderness. The result was that his madness returned. Suibne and the old woman leaped like birds from tree to tree. The incoherence of the dialogue between Suibne and the old woman is probably intentional and meant to convey his madness.

There are two versions of Suibne's death, which he himself prophesies at the end of this poem. In one a cowherd slays him with a spear. In the other the cowherd places the tip of a deer's horn in such a position that it pierces Suibne when he bends to drink.

Rónán Finn: The saint whose curse caused Suibne to go mad at the battle of Mag Rath (A.D. 639). He died in A.D. 664.

Congal Cláen: King of the Ulaid in east Ulster. He had given Suibne the cloak he wore into battle. Congal was slain there.

Mag Coba: A plain in southwest county Down.

Carn Cornáin: A hill somewhere in eastern Ulster.

Slíab Níad: A place on the way from Carn Cornáin to the south of Ireland.

Galtee Mountains: In county Tipperary.

Lorc's Carn Liffe: Lorc was a legendary king of Leinster.

Carn Liffe: A hill, probably near the Liffey Valley, counties Kildare and Dublin.

Gort's Binbulbin: A peak in the Mourne Mountains.

Glenn Bolcáin: A glen somewhere in the north of Ireland. See note to "The Cry of the Garb."

Colmán: Father of Suibne.

Lugaid: Cell Lugaid, an unidentified monastery.

Line: Old Irish name for Moylinny, a place in county Antrim. I used it for the sake of the meter.

Slieve Phelim: A place on the border of county Tipperary and northern county Limerick.

Fews: Mountains in county Armagh.

Duhallow: In county Cork.

Orrery: In county Cork.

Lough Leane: In county Kerry.

Island Magee: In county Antrim.

Cunghill: In county Cork.

Burren: In county Kerry

"Antler Man": Old Irish *Fer Benn* means "man of peaks" or "man of antlers."

Layd: Perhaps the Layd of county Antrim.

Dún Máil: An unidentified place.

Taídiu: A watercourse bringing water from the Glenn River to Mo Ling's monastery, south county Carlow.

Suibne in the Snow

Mourne Mountains: County Down.

Aughty Mountains: On the border of counties Clare and Galway.

Gáille: A district in east Connacht.

Kerry Stacks: Probably the stacks on the Glanaruddery Mountains, county Kerry.

Glenn Bolcáin: See note to "The Cry of the Garb."

Moylinny: A place in county Antrim.

Mag Lí: A plain in county Derry, west of the river Bann.

Liffey Valley: A place in counties Kildare and Dublin.

Segas: A place in the Fews Mountains, county Armagh.

Rathmore: A place in Moylinny.

Mag nAí: A plain in county Roscommon.

Plains of Boyle: In county Roscommon.

Crúachán: A number of places have this name.

Knockmealdown Mountains: In county Waterford.

Slieve Brey: In county Louth.

Cáel Praises Créide's House

From "The Colloquy of Ancient Men," which includes more than two hundred anecdotes supposed to have been related by Caílte or Oisín, ancient survivors of Finn's third-century Fíana, to Saint Patrick and others in the fifth century. The poem dates to about A.D. 1175.

The prose that precedes this poem tells of Créide's coming with 150 women to receive the Fían chieftain. He said that he had come to woo her for Cáel. Créide asked if he had a poem for her, whereupon Cáel recited these verses.

Finn was a legendary pagan hero whose war bands were called Fíana. They were on the whole seen as a force for good. They drove marauders, monsters, many beasts, and bands of exiles from Ireland. Once during a plague they fed all the people of Ireland and put seven cows and a bull in every farmstead. One notable thing about them was that they fought always on foot.

Cáel: Seems to have been king of Leister and a member of Finn's Fíana.

Créide: Otherworld daughter of Cairbre.

"Worried I travel on Friday": In Ireland and Gaelic Scotland today Friday is thought to be an unlucky day for beginning things.

Paps Mountains: In east county Kerry.

Tuile: The name of a legendary craftsman.

Cairbre: The father of Créide and king of Cíarraige Lúachra.

Tulcha Trí mBenn: Hills of Three Peaks. An unidentified place but probably in county Kerry.

Créide's Lament for Cáel

This poem is also a part of the Finn Cycle. It dates to about A.D. 1175.

Créide: See notes on preceding poem.

Cáel: See notes on preceding poem.

Reenverc: In county Kerry.

Loch Dá Chonn: A lake, probably in Leinster.

Drumkeen: In county Kerry.

Leiter Laíg: An unidentified place.

Drumlesh: Old Irish *Druim Dú Léis*. Perhaps modern Drumlesh, county Clare.

Druim Sílenn: An unidentified place.

Daire Dá Dos: An unidentified place.

Tulach Léis: An unidentified hill, perhaps in west county Kerry.

Crimthan: King of Leinster and father of Cáel.

The prose following this poem tells of Créide's lying down at Cáel's side and dying of grief for him. They were buried in the same tomb.

Description of Winter

This poem dates to about A.D. 1175.

Slievecarran: In county Clare.

Caílte: A member of the Fíana and reciter of this poem.

Díarmait: A member of Finn's Fíana.

Oscar: Son of Oisín and a member of Finn's Fíana.

Corann: In county Sligo.

Tuns: Old Irish *Tonn Túaige* (Wave of Túag), in Dundrum Bay, county Down.

May Day

Finn learned the three arts that established him as a poet: prophetic marrow chewing, divination that illuminates, and incantation from heads. He composed this poem to prove his skill. The poem appears in a corrupt manuscript of the fifteenth century, but the language is that of the ninth century.

Summer Has Gone

This poem is attributed to Finn. It dates to the ninth or tenth century A.D.

Gráinne Speaks of Díarmait

Gráinne was the daughter of Cormac. She eloped with Díarmait after having been promised to Finn. She is said to have spoken these words to Finn. Díarmait was a member of Finn's Fíana.

These Hands Are Withered

This poem is attributed to the legendary Oisín, son of Finn. It dates to about A.D. 1100.

Once I Had Golden Curls

This poem too is ascribed to Oisín. It dates to about A.D. 1200.